'TILL DEATH DO US PART:

DEADLY DIVORCES:

WHEN MARRIAGE ENDS IN MURDER

MURDER IN THE FAMILY SERIES

SYLVIA PERRINI

TABLE OF CONTENTS

INTRODUCTION

Every year, over two million people make the decision to get married. For many people, it's the happiest day of their lives. After all they are combining two separate lives and making them into one. But what happens after the cake is cut and the guests go home? For a lot of people, they start planning their families, their careers, and their mutual goals. For others, however, once the honeymoon is over, reality sets in and they are able to see for themselves that maybe marriage isn't all that it's cracked up to be. Or the person they married wasn`t who they wanted to spend the rest of their lives with after all.

When people decide they cannot live together anymore, it often ends up in divorce. In fact, over one million people get divorced each year. The reasons for divorce are as individualized as the people experiencing them; however, some of the more common reasons include money, disagreement over kids, adultery, and simply growing apart. Nearly fifty per cent of the people who get married, will end up in divorce. It may seem like a harsh statistic, but it's much better than the alternative.

Every year, a handful of people decide that divorce is simply not enough. Instead of choosing to end their marriage and go their separate ways, people decide to take measures into their own hands. The result: murder. Each year, a few thousand people are lost to murder at the hands of their spouses or significant others. In fact, for married women it is one of the leading causes of death. For pregnant women, homicide is the leading cause of death. It's scary to think about, but unfortunately it happens more often than you might expect.

In several cases, it's just a matter of one

spouse or the other being heartbroken over losing who they thought was the love of their life. When they took their vows, they meant they would not be apart until death. And they took that meaning quite literally. In other cases, it's a matter of revenge due to infidelity or other ways a spouse felt wronged. They feel they have to take back what's rightfully theirs, or at least make it so no one else can have it, either.

In some of the more extreme cases, it has to do with child custody. Child custody battles can get notoriously heated, with both sides usually wanting to have as much of their children as possible. It's often during custody situations where a person's harshest personality comes out. They fling blame at the other person and list all of the reasons they should not have access to their children. After hearing all of these unkind things, it's understandable that a person would be upset. Sometimes, that culminates into murder.

In terms of pregnant women, it's often because the other half of the couple did not want children in the first place. For a lot of men, having children is a scary prospect. After all, they have to give up their freedom and be responsible for another human life. It can be daunting and overwhelming. Many people simply don't know how to handle that kind of situation. Some men choose to leave their pregnant wives or girlfriends, others choose to go a more permanent and deadly route.

When someone is murdered, the spouse is usually the very first place people look. Most of the time, it's because they did it; however, there are cases, that despite the overwhelming evidence against them, they still manage to walk away with a not guilty verdict. Take the O.J. Simpson case, for example. If you were to stop people on the street and ask them if they thought O.J. was guilty of murdering Nicole Brown or Ronald Goldman, you would probably get an overwhelming yes. Despite this, he was acquitted of all his charges and the case technically remains unsolved.

By taking a look at these fascinating, interesting, and deadly cases, it might shed some light as to why people choose to murder instead of taking the less lethal routes of divorce. What might be surprising are the genders involved. When people think of a deadly divorce, they tend to think of a man murdering his wife; however, a lot of times the woman is the one that finally snaps. She could be jilted because her husband left her, angry about an affair, or feel she is owed more money than what was allotted to her in the divorce decree.

Whether the act was committed by a man or a woman, one thing is painfully clear: by looking at the signs, many of these murders could have been prevented. Before a person commits an act as heinous as murder, there are usually warnings. They are either unstable, have a history of abuse, or even have a history of threats and stalking. If people would take these sorts of instances seriously, several lives could perhaps be saved.

RUTH SNYDER

Ruth Snyder, a tall, attractive blonde coupled with a strong personality, was trapped in a loveless marriage – or so she claimed. Her husband, Albert, was the art editor of a Motor Boating magazine, and frequently worked long hours. Instead of leaving her husband, however, Ruth decided to take on an additional lover. A married salesman named Henry "Judd" Gray. This might not seem like such an unusual story, except for the fact that this happened in the mid-1920s. At the time, this type of situation was quite scandalous.

Nonetheless, at some point during her relationship with Judd, Ruth decided she wanted her husband dead and gone. She began telling Judd of her alleged abuse at the hands of her husband. Over and over again, she claimed he should be killed in order for her to be able to live her life. At first, Judd was unwilling to go along with this plan; however, Ruth was quite persuasive and managed to convince Judd that ending her husband's life was the right thing to do.

Therefore, on March 19, 1927, Judd slipped into the couple's bedroom, in Queens, New York City, with the help of Ruth. Judd, once in the bedroom, grabbed a nearby weight and brought it down on to Albert's head. There was no power behind the attack, and soon Albert was awake and fighting back. Judd, who was much smaller than Albert, quickly ended up on the losing side of this and he was pinned to the ground. Ruth, forced to take matters into her own hands, grabbed the weight and, while he was distracted fighting Judd, swung it against Albert's head – killing him.

After the attack was over and Albert was

dead on the ground, Judd fled upstate to the city of Syracuse. Meanwhile Ruth, who pretended to have been tied up, awakened her and Albert's nine year old daughter, Lorraine, and sent her to get help for a burglary that had ended in murder.

As soon as the police arrived at the Snyder´s home, however, they noticed that the story didn't seem to add up. There were no signs of forced entry and all of the items Ruth claimed were stolen were found on the property – but hidden. Once the police started questioning Ruth about the items, she slipped up and mentioned Judd. While the police weren't initially suspicious of him, they certainly were now.

Judd, for his part, tried to claim he was in a hotel room several hours away at the time of the murder. Deeper investigation, however, revealed a friend of his had set up the room for him as an alibi. When he was confronted with the evidence, Judd came clean, detailing both his and Ruth's involvement in the murder – resulting in both of their arrests.

Motive

As more information came out, it turned out the love triangle was not the only reason Ruth wanted her husband dead. For the entirety of Ruth's marriage to Albert, he was still infatuated with Jessie Guishard, his late deceased fiancée. In fact, he talked about her all of the time, making Ruth feel insecure in her own marriage. On top of that, Albert kept a few of his fiancée's artifacts around and named his boat after her. A decision that likely did not sit well with Ruth.

On top of that, it was discovered Ruth took out a $48,000 life insurance policy on her husband – one that the insurance agent signed fraudulently. As if that weren't enough, she put on an addendum that would pay her double if he were met with a violent and sudden death. It has since come out that Ruth had tried to kill her husband no less than seven times before she ultimately succeeded.

Ruth Snyder Mug Shot

Trial and Aftermath

The trial was fairly straightforward, as both Ruth and Judd had confessed, at least in part, to killing Albert. The jury took less than two hours to find them both guilty and sentence them to death. It was a decision that shocked both of them. Ruth most likely thought she would escape the death penalty due to her gender and the fact that a woman had not been executed in New York since 1899. Judd probably figured since Ruth was the one that did the fatal blow, he would face less time.

Alas, on January 12, 1928, Judd faced the electric chair. Before he died, he claimed his wife had forgiven him and he was no longer afraid of death. Therefore, when he was executed, it was reported he died with a smile on his face.

Ruth Snyder on death row in Sing Sing prison, N.Y.

The jailer then went to get Ruth, and he later reported she knew it was her turn when she saw the lights of the jail flicker, signaling Judd's death. She, too, claimed she had been forgiven, but by God. As with Judd, she accepted her fate and died a few minutes after she was strapped into the electric chair.

A reporter covering the story managed to sneak in a camera and snapped a picture of Ruth strapped into the electric chair and printed it the following day in the New York Daily News. It is a haunting image that stuck in many people's minds long after the fact. Many of the people of the 1920s lived for this kind of scandal, so seeing a woman strapped into the chair, taking her last few breaths, kept interest in her case for decades.

Following the pronouncement of the death sentence on Ruth, many legal arguments took place between the various relatives of both Ruth and Albert Snyder concerning the care of their daughter Lorraine. Albert Snyder`s brother, petitioned the court to be allowed to appoint a legal guardian who was not a member of Ruth Snyder's family. Ruth Snyder mother, Josephine Brown, petitioned the court for custody of Lorraine who had been living with her since Ruth´s arrest.

Josephine Brown was awarded guardianship of Lorraine on September 7, 1927.

CLAUS AND SUNNY VON BULOW

Perhaps one of the oddest cases of a potentially deadly divorce is the attempted murder of Sunny Von Bülow. She had grown up in privilege, having inherited over 100 million dollars when she was just four years old, due to her father's death. Sunny was born Martha Crawford, but was given the nickname due to her cheerful disposition.

She grew up attractive and popular; many guys wanted to be with her, but she ended up meeting and then marrying Alfred Eduard Fredrich Vincenz Martin Maria Prince von Auersperg. If that name sounds like a mouthful, it's because he was the son of an Austrian prince. The two were married for eight years and had two children together, Ala and Alexander, before they divorced in 1965. Alfred ended up dying from injuries resulting from a car accident in 1983.

Just over a year after her divorce from Alfred, Sunny met and then married Danish born Claus Von Bülow. After a dozen years of marriage, and one daughter, Cosima, the two had grown distant from each other. They were both clearly unhappy in the marriage, but neither one started to speak of divorce until the middle of 1979.

Sunny and Claus Von Bulow

Claus spent much time in New York, spending time in Sunny's deluxe Fifth Avenue apartment. Whilst in New York, he was openly conducting an affair with Alexandra Isles, a stunningly attractive Swedish actress.

Odd Incidents

The day after Christmas in 1979, family members arrived to Sunny's house to find her on the ground and unresponsive. They took her to the hospital where she lingered in a coma several days before finally coming out of it and being revived. After several rounds of testing, the doctors determined Sunny had problems controlling her blood sugar and warned her to watch her sugar intake and be careful with her insulin injections.

A few months later, in April of 1980, the same thing happened. Sunny was found unresponsive and rushed to the hospital. This time, doctors diagnosed her as hypoglycemic and said again if she ate too much sugar, failed to properly take her insulin, or indulged in alcohol, it could mean dire consequences.

Finally, in December of 1980, almost exactly a full year after the first incident, family members went over to Sunny's house for a holiday celebration. During the party, Sunny went into the restroom and passed out. Once again, her family rushed her to the emergency room. This time, even though Sunny remained alive, she would be in a vegetative state. She remained in that state for over two dozen years before dying.

Claus von Bülow

When the first incident happened, no one suspected Claus of having anything to do with trying to hurt or murder his estranged wife. By the time the second and then the third came around, more and more people were starting to have their suspicions, including Sunny's children. They knew Sunny and Claus were having problems and thought he may have been after her fortune. Police officials, after performing their own investigation, agreed and arrested Claus von Bülow in July of 1981 and charged him with two counts of attempted murder.

The trial, though widely watched, went about as smoothly as can be expected. Even though Claus maintained his innocence, the prosecution had dozens of witnesses and experts willing to take the stand against him. This included the actress Alexandra Isles, who testified that she had given Claus an ultimatum that she would end their relationship unless he separated from Sunny. Even though there wasn't any direct evidence linking Claus to the murder, the prosecution still felt they had enough to convict him. It turns out, they were right; when the case was turned over to the jury in 1982, after nearly five days of deliberation, they found him guilty of both charges.

Claus, was allowed to remain out on his $100,000 bail until sentencing.

A little more than a month later, Von Bülow was sentenced to ten years in prison on the first count, in which Sunny had recovered. For the second count of the irreversible coma, Claus was sentenced to 20 years. The Judge, however, allowed him to remain free on $1 million bond pending an appeal.

Claus immediately set about hiring the best attorneys money could buy to appeal his case. And the case went back to trial. This time, the defence was more prepared with experts of their own. They put several doctors and scientists on the stand who all testified on behalf of Claus. They claimed it was impossible for insulin to cause the kind of coma Sunny was in and it may have been caused by taking recreational drugs.

Alexandra Isles again testified and in this trial contended that Mr. von Bülow had described to her how he had watched his wife slip into the first coma, decided not to call a doctor but later summoned aid.

Despite this testimony, the jury felt there was enough reasonable doubt to overturn Claus' conviction. He was free to go. Even though Claus has continued to maintain his innocence, most of his family has turned against him. Everyone in Sunny's family, except his daughter Cosima, is convinced he did, in fact, try to murder her for her money and public opinion is still very much divided.

Aftermath

Because Cosima had stood by her father, her maternal grandmother, Annie Laurie

Crawford Aitken who controlled all of the family money, disinherited her grand-daughter in case she might funnel money to her father. When Annie Aitken died in 1984, Cosima von Bülow filed a lawsuit claiming that family members had turned her grandmother against her and requested that her rights to her inheritance be reinstated.

The two attempted murder trials of Claus von Bülow were amongst the most sensational of the 1980s. News media from all around the world were fascinated by the drama of the beautiful million dollar heiress who lay like a sleeping beauty in a twilight zone, the debonair husband accused of attempted murder, his attractive mistress and two royal children pitted against their younger half sister, with the dazzling social circles of New York and Newport providing the backdrop.

The court room trials became the subject matter of the 1990 movie "Reversal of Fortune" with Jeremy Irons as Claus von Bülow and Glenn Close as Sunny von Bülow. Sunny´s eldest daughter, Princess Annie Laurie von Auersperg said the movie was a "commercialization of a tragedy."

On July 19th, 1985, the stepchildren of Claus von Bülow filed a $56 million civil suit against him. At the time Claus stood to inherit $14 million of his wife's estate, estimated at $75 million.

The suit stated that Mr. von Bülow *''sought to obtain assets worth millions of dollars by secretly scheming to defraud and murder his wife.''*

The suit further alleged that in December 1979 Mr. von Bülow injected his wife with insulin at their Rhodes Island mansion, causing her to lapse into a coma. It further alleged that on that night and the next day, the: *''Defendant did nothing to help his wife. Instead, he actively took steps to conceal her condition and made misleading statements to those, including a doctor, who might otherwise have come to her aid. Defendant refused to call a doctor to attend to his wife until, despite his efforts at concealment, her condition became apparent to others who demanded that a doctor be summoned.''*

Sunny von Bülow recovered but fell into the second coma on December. 27, 1980. The suit alleged the second coma came after Claus von Bülow once again injected his wife with insulin "and other drugs, alone or in combination."

The suit further declared that the;

''Defendant should be declared to have no entitlement to safekeeping, support or maintenance by Martha von Bülow or by people acting for her." At the time Claus von Bülow was living in his wife's luxurious Fifth Avenue apartment in New York.

The civil lawsuit was eventually settled out-of-court in 1987. In the settlement Claus von Bülow agreed to his step-children´s demands and divorce their comatose mother and to give up all claims to her fortune and his yearly trust-fund income settled on him during the early years of his marriage to Sunny. It was further stipulated that Mr. von Bülow was to never discuss the case publicly and refuse any rights to book or movie deals about the family's feuding.

Claus agreed to the demands in return that his daughter Cosima, inherited an equal share of her maternal grandmother Annie Aitken's estate (estimated to be around $48 million.)

Claus and Sunny were divorced in 1988.

Claus von Bülow then moved to London where he began work as an art and theatre critic. He became a much-loved figure among the wealthy cocktail party set. Annabel Goldsmith, the London society hostess thinks him so kind and gentle that she calls him 'Clausikins'. And in her book, *The Pelham Cottage Years*, she talks about his generosity with Beluga caviar and his weakness for handmade shoes. In 2001, he was voted as the 46th 'most invited' party guest in London by the society magazine, *Tatler*.

When Cosima graduated from university in the U.S, she then moved to London to be close to her father. She has since married an Italian count, Riccardo Pavoncelli, and they live just around the corner from her father in Knightsbridge with their three children.

Sunny remained in a coma, curled up in a fetal position, for twenty-eight years. She died in December 2008, aged 76, without ever regaining consciousness, taking with her to the grave the secret of her comatose condition. During all that time, her children regularly visited her, and would spend time by her bed chatting to her about their lives and children, and desperately hoping, to the end, she would regain consciousness.

Her doctor testified in court, that the cost of maintaining Sunny in her comatose state was around $375,000 the first year. By the end of her life, it was estimated that the cost of her treatment to her family, including the expenses of a security guard, was around $1, 2 million a year.

NATALIE WOOD

Natalie Wood was a huge movie star in the late 1950s and 1960s. She started acting around the age of four, and got her big break when she was eight years old and landed a starring role in Miracle on 34th Street. After that, she starred in many movies, including Gypsy, Rebel Without a Cause, and West Side Story. She was a Hollywood darling and extremely talented; earning three Oscar nomination before she was twenty-five years old.

Natalie Wood in Splendor in the Grass, 1961

After a successful movie and television career, Natalie took some time away from acting to focus on her children. Even though she remained devoted to her kids, she had trouble keeping her marriage together. She married Robert Wagner two times, and married Richard Gregson in between her marriages to Robert. Despite her personal life being odd and hard to maintain, she always put on a brave face to the public.

Natalie Wood in 1973

In the early 1980s, Natalie wanted to resume her movie career and took on a lead role opposite Christopher Walken in a movie called Brainstorm. It was during the making of that film that tragedy struck. When Natalie was only 43 years old, she drowned in California. For years, her death was ruled an accident. After prodding from her family, and other outside sources, the cause of death was changed to undetermined.

Natalie Wood and Robert Wagner in 1975

Natalie drowned while she was on a boat trip with Robert Wagner and Christopher Walken. No one saw Natalie enter the water, which is why there has been so much mystery surrounding the event. When Natalie's body was recovered, some cuts and bruises were found on her face and arms; but investigators couldn't establish how or when they were received. In addition, an autopsy revealed Natalie had been drinking the night she drowned, and had also taken some pills which increased the effects of the alcohol in her system. These factors caused the official cause of death to be listed as an accident.

Thirty years later in 2011, the captain of the boat on that fateful night stepped forward with some new information. He stated Natalie and Robert had been fighting that evening. Upon further investigation, there were recordings made of the two of them that also alluded to these new details that had been brought to the police's attention.

Even though the world may never know what, exactly, happened to Natalie Wood on the night of her death, her husband is considered to be a suspect, or at least a person of interest. Due to thirty years of time, and the fact that water washes away a lot of evidence, it is unlikely he will ever be brought to trial to account for her murder, if that was what it was.

JIM AND LITA SULLIVAN

When Lita and Jim met each other in the mid 70´s, it was love at first sight. They were both attractive, well-spoken, and witty. Not to mention, Jim was extremely rich; a factor that may have only added to Lita's growing fondness for him. The two dated for a while, and ultimately decided to get married. Jim, however, was harboring a secret – he had been married once before and had four children. He decided not to let Lita in on this fact until the night before they were due to be wed in December 1976. Lita, though understandably surprised, decided to go through with the marriage with Jim. She loved him and she was willing to overlook that tiny detail about his life.

Just after the wedding, the couple moved

to Georgia, which made Lita's parents uneasy. Lita was African-American and they worried about her in the "Deep South". Also, they felt Jim wasn't a good pick for a spouse because he lied about his ex-wife and his children – so what else might he be hiding? Lita chose to ignore her parents' concerns and the two of them seemed happy, for a while.

Even though they were wealthy in Georgia, Lita always felt uneasy due to her race. Many in the community frowned upon interracial marriages. When Jim sold his company for five million dollars, they figured it was the perfect time to move to a more accepting community and ended up in Palm Beach, Florida. Here they purchased a spectacular villa overlooking the ocean. Their dream of climbing the social ladder was not to be realized, however, as many people in the high society in Palm Beach, also shunned the couple because of Lita's race.

Jim, who wanted more than anything to be accepted among the rich and social elite, blamed Lita for not being able to achieve his dream and started dating other women behind her back. When Lita learned of the affairs, she tried desperately to save her marriage. After several attempts, however, Lita realized it simply wouldn't be possible and moved back home with her family and filed for divorce. Even though the marriage was over, Lita still hoped to retain some of the fortune Jim had acquired during their marriage.

The Murder

One day in early 1987, Lita was home by herself when there was a knock at the door. When she opened it, there was a man standing on the step with a flower delivery for her. As Lita reached to take the flowers from him, the man pulled out a gun and shot at her. One of the shots hit her head and she crumbled to the ground; the delivery man fled. A neighbor heard the shots and immediately called the authorities. When they got to the house, they found Lita still alive. They rushed her to the hospital and the doctors tried to save her life. It was not to be, however, and Lita died from her injuries.

Lita Sullivan

After the murder, Jim Sullivan became a prime suspect, but the investigators had trouble linking him to the actual crime. The man who delivered the flowers to Lita was decidedly not

Jim; however, police officers believed Jim had hired him. All they needed to do was prove it.

When the authorities questioned Jim, he claimed not to know anything about what had happened and said he had nothing to do with it. In fact, he suggested Lita was using drugs and it was simply a drug deal that had gone terribly wrong. Jim's closest supporters may have bought this story, but no one who knew Lita, nor the authorities, did. They gained access to his phone records and discovered someone called him from the area Lita had been shot just a few minutes after the crime had been committed. Another day, while police were tracing phone calls, Jim mentioned the type of gun that had been used to kill Lita; a fact police deliberately withheld. Investigators were now convinced they had their man, but they still lacked enough evidence to prove it.

Another Marriage, Another Divorce

Just eight months after Lita's death, Jim married a woman named Suki. She was young, beautiful, and well-connected. With Suki at his side, Jim climbed the social ranks of Palm Beach's high society. He was thrilled to finally be accepted and loved his new lifestyle. Things started to unravel for him, however, when he was pulled over for a routine traffic stop. He was supposed to go to traffic court, but convinced Suki to take his place instead. At the trial, she said she was the one driving and the officer made a mistake. The judge didn't buy it and sentenced Jim to one year of house arrest for perjury.

While he was serving his one-year sentence, authorities did a routine search of the house. Inside, they found four guns, which was a violation of the order against him. After learning of this, the judge tacked on an additional year and a half onto his sentence. During this, Suki decided she simply couldn't stay with Jim anymore and filed for divorce. The couple soon turned against each other, each growing bitter and petty. Suki then went to the police and claimed Jim confessed to murdering Lita; she said she was afraid for her own life and wanted someone to know because she didn't want to be next. Finally, the authorities had what they needed and traveled to Florida to arrest Jim and extradite him back to Atlanta to stand trial for the murder of Lita.

The Trials

During the trial, the prosecution told their side of the story, but were unable to come up with any concrete proof linking Jim Sullivan to the murder. Also, even though Suki testified against Jim, the defense shot down her credibility. They claimed she was a bitter ex-wife who was simply trying to get back at Jim for all of the problems in their marriage. It turned into a case of he-said, she-said. The judge, having listened to both sides, chose to dismiss the case due to lack of evidence.

Jim was thrilled with this outcome and immediately returned to West Palm Beach. The society, however, was unwilling to take him back. He lost his prestige, his spot on the committees he served, and most of his friends. Heartbroken and angry, he sold his Palm Beach house and bought a ranch in nearby Boynton Beach.

For a while the case seemed to be unsolvable, with Jim escaping his fate at every turn. Finally, after a few years, Lita's case aired on one of the unsolved crime shows. Someone recognized Jim Sullivan as the man who paid her boyfriend, Phillip Harwood, to kill Lita.

Police wasted no time in tracking Phillip down, and when they did, it only took a few minutes of questioning for him to confess everything. Phillip said Jim had offered him $25,000 to kill Lita, which he subsequently did. The police arrested Phillip and then turned their sights on Jim, finally feeling as though they finally had enough evidence to convict him of murdering his ex-wife.

Finally, in May 1998, 13 years after Lita had been murdered, an arrest warrant was issued for Jim´s arrest. He must have suspected the authorities were closing in on him, because when they went to arrest him, they discovered he had fled to Costa Rica. Over the next few years, Jim traveled around South America, Europe, and finally ended up in Thailand. While he was there, he married a new woman and had started a life with her. in July 2002 Thai police arrested him at a resort community, Cha-am, 100 miles (170 km) south of Bangkok. 19 months later, he was extradited back to the United States to stand trial for the murder of Lita Sullivan.

Nineteen years after Lita's grisly murder Jim´s trial began in February of 2006. The prosecution had found several witnesses tied directly to the murder that were willing to testify against Jim. Phillip, the flower delivery guy who actually committed the crime, plead down from the death penalty to twenty years to life in exchange for his testimony.

The case was eventually turned over to the jury, who took less than five hours to deliberate. They came back with a verdict: Jim Sullivan was found guilty of first degree murder and sentenced to life in prison. Finally, nearly twenty years after Lita died, Jim Sullivan was brought to justice and there was some closure for her family.

BETTY BRODERICK

Betty grew up in the 1950s and 60s to a typical working class family. She went to a Catholic school and had a pretty normal childhood. After high school, she went to a nearby college and earned a degree; something her family encouraged.

When Betty was seventeen years old, she met Dan Broderick while she was on a weekend retreat with some friends of hers. She was instantly smitten with him and the two of them began a relationship. He would travel from Cornell Medical School to visit her and spend time with her family. It seemed the two of them were a match made in heaven; they both valued education, both came from respectable Catholic families, and even shared similar taste in music.

Betty and Dan on their wedding day.

On April 12, 1969, the two were married in Eastchester, N.Y. Shortly after they returned from their honeymoon in the Caribbean Betty learned she was pregnant with their first child, daughter Kim. During the course of their marriage Betty gave birth to four more children: two sons named Daniel and Rhett, another daughter, Lee, and another boy, who died two days after birth.

For a while, the two of them struggled to make ends meet. Betty worked multiple jobs to help support the family while Dan finished up medical school. Dan, however, decided medicine was not the place for him, and entered into law school in Massachusetts. While he was there, he excelled, but decided he would have a better shot at getting a good job if he moved to California. Once again, the family picked up and moved across the country. There, Dan was able to get a job as a junior attorney fresh out of school.

In a few years, it all paid off, and Betty was able to be a wife and mother while Dan worked. It was an arrangement that seemingly made them both happy. And to everyone who knew them, they were a happy couple with a great little family.

Problems at Home

Even though the couple presented a pretty picture to the outside world, behind closed doors, things were not always what they seemed. Dan was climbing the ladder at work, and became obsessed with the prospect of earning more money. As such, he worked late hours and attended many social functions he believed he was expected to be at to gain contacts in his field. Betty, for her part, missed her husband, but didn't speak up, believing Dan was doing what he thought was best for his family.

There were also definite inequalities in the state of their marriage. For example, Dan spent most weekends with his fraternity brothers, while Betty was expected to sit at home with the children and wait for him. Also, Dan would buy himself the finest clothes and cars while Betty shopped at the discount stores and received hand-me-downs. Even appliances she had to beg her husband to buy. For years she washed her clothes at the Laundromat because Dan wouldn't buy her a washer or a dryer.

Eventually, Dan came around and started treated Betty like the other corporate wives. He stopped spending time at the bar and spent time with her instead. He included her in decisions and even got her into the country club so she could socialize with other women. Dan even hired a maid to help Betty out around the house. At first, Betty was thrilled with the sudden change of heart.

As the couple got more money, it seemed their problems grew. They often accused the other of overspending and buying frivolous objects. Stemming from their problems, Dan began to spend less time with Betty and more time at the bar. In time, Betty grew afraid of Dan. Even the maid noticed how Betty's normally happy demeanor would change when it neared the time for Dan to arrive home.

Eventually, Dan's eye began to wander; he started spending time with a young woman named Linda. He had met her at a party he attended with Betty and immediately felt an attraction. Dan ended up tracking the twenty-one year old Linda down and then hired her to be his personal assistant, despite the fact that she had no paralegal training nor could she even type. He was all about maintaining his rich, beautiful image, and he felt Linda was a perfect part of that.

Even though Betty was suspicious, she held her emotions in check until she had some more concrete proof. Betty ignored the late night phone calls, and the fact that Dan sent flowers to his new assistant. One day, determined to see for herself what Dan was up to, Betty went over to the office but found both Dan and Linda's offices empty. She waited around for most of the afternoon, but they never came back. Enraged, Betty raced home, grabbed Dan's expensive wardrobe, and set it on fire in the backyard. Dan, continued to deny that he was having an affair with Linda. But eventually, the affair led to Betty and Dan´s separation.

Dan moved out of the rental home they were living in at the time and moved back to the family home that they were having renovated. He was supposed to pay her alimony and child support, but only sent her a small amount of money every now and again. Also, he pretty much wanted nothing to do with his children. Only when Betty insisted he see them did he spend any time with them at all. On top of that, he never broke off the affair, still continuing to see Linda, and eventually moving her into what had been his and Betty´s home.

Upping the Ante

Betty became more unhinged the longer she and Dan were separated, and noticeably more so when he filed for divorce. One day, when she visited her former home, she noticed a Boston Crème Pie on the counter. She took the pie and threw chocolate all over Dan and Linda´s bed and clothes, ruining a lot of them in the process. In response, Dan got a restraining order against Betty.

Source: Google

Dan and Linda

Betty, however, was having none of that. Instead of listening to the order, she went around to the house again and threw a bottle of wine through the window. When Dan called the police, they refused to get involved, claiming it was simply a dispute between two spouses.

Since Dan was a successful lawyer in their

area, Betty had to go several counties away to find a successful lawyer to handle her side of the divorce. Her lawyer warned her time and time again to leave Dan alone, but she wouldn't listen. She continued to slight Dan in front of the kids and destroy his property. Among other things, she broke a toaster, a mirror, the answering machine, the wallpaper, and a stereo, usually in the presence of their children. On Christmas Eve of 1985, she broke into Dan and Linda's house and destroyed all of the Christmas presents before smashing a mirror and leaving. Her attorney almost removed himself from the case, saying she needed to control her behavior if she wanted representation. Betty agreed, but had no intention of following through.

Over the next several years, Betty continued to antagonize Dan and Linda. Dan even moved from the house he and Betty had once shared to a brand new house nearby at one point to get rid of Betty once and for all, but she followed him and became even crazier. The final straw for Dan came when Betty actually drove a car through the front door of his brand new house, shattering the frame. The police came and got Betty and took her to a mental institution so she could calm down for a few days. Dan, seizing his opportunity, officially finalized the divorce papers.

Since Dan was a successful attorney, he was one step ahead of Betty for the entire time. Every move she tried to make, Dan would shut down. Over time, Betty grew increasingly frustrated because she was outmatched legally, but felt she had no choice. Trying to help herself, she fired her attorney and tried to fight Dan on her own. When she failed to show up for the court date, however, the judge awarded everything, including custody of the children, to Dan.

Even though he wasn't her lawyer anymore, the attorney that had been representing Betty petitioned the court on her behalf. He said it wasn't fair that Dan had a lock on all of the attorneys in the area because of his connections and Betty deserved to have a competent lawyer on her side. Dan, to his credit, agreed with this and even paid for Betty's new representation. Over time, however, the new lawyer removed himself from her case. Betty was forced to represent herself, and it didn't go well. The judge saw how unhinged she was and still awarded Dan everything he had been seeking. On top of that, Linda and Dan decided to marry – an act that would prove to be the final straw for Betty.

The Murders

In the wee hours of the morning on November 5, 1989, Betty woke up, grabbed a gun, and tiptoed out of the apartment in which she now lived. She drove over to Linda and

Dan's house and sneaked in through the back door. Since she had been to the house to vandalize it on numerous occasions, she knew exactly where to go.

Betty crept through the house until she found the couple's bedroom. She opened the door and shot at Dan and Linda until they were both dead from their wounds. Betty then turned herself into the police, claiming she was in a haze and didn't quite know what happened, only that Dan and Linda were dead and that it was somehow her fault.

By the time the trial rolled around, the nation was hooked on Betty's story. She granted interviews to whoever asked, because she wanted to present her side of the story to the public at large. She felt this would gain her more sympathy and people just might understand why she did what she did. While this was going on, the prosecutors wanted to make sure they would win their case and not be seen picking on someone who had already been through enough; therefore, they decided not to seek the death penalty.

Even though Betty had confessed to murdering Dan and Linda, the question of whether or not it was premeditated hung in the air. In fact, by the time the case was passed to the jury, they couldn't make a decision, either. They came back with no verdict because they could not come to a unanimous consensus.

The second trial, however, went much smoother than the first one. The prosecution was much more prepared and they were able to poke holes in nearly all of the defense's arguments. Also, the judge didn't believe Betty had been abused throughout her marriage to Dan, and refused to allow any testimony that would allude to such. This time, the jury came back with a verdict: second degree murder. Betty was sentenced to thirty-two years to life in prison. She is due to be released in 2021.

Betty, who has been in prison since the day of the murders, said during the early days of her incarceration that she felt safe in prison and that it was the first time in a long time she hadn´t felt afraid. She said she liked the stability and the routine prison life had to offer.

In January 2010, Betty, aged 62, had her first parole hearing. The Parole Board, after a five hour hearing, denied her parole as they said she showed no remorse and did not admit wrongdoing. Her four children attended the hearing and were divided on whether she should be set free. Two of them asked the board to release their mother, whilst the other two requested the board to keep her in prison.

PAMELA SMART

Pam Smart is one of the most notorious women in recent history. She started an affair with a fifteen year old student and then convinced him and his friends to kill her husband in order to continue their relationship. This case had the nation riveted for several weeks as they tried to piece together exactly what happened and who was responsible.

Early Life

Pamela Smart was a typical young girl. She made good grades and was a cheerleader in high school. She had a lot of friends and seemed to have a happy childhood. After being accepted into Florida State University, she graduated with a communications degree in just three years. While she was there, she hosted a few radios shows on the campus' college radio station. It turned out to be something she was very good at, and loved to do, because she got to show off her knowledge and love of heavy metal music and still broadcast over the airwaves.

Also while in school, Pamela met Gregory Smart and the two of them hit it off. Just before they graduated, the two of them married. After graduation, they decided to relocate to New Hampshire, where Pamela took a job as the media coordinator at a local high school. While she was there, she became involved in a program called "Project Self-Esteem" for troubled youths. It was to promote drug awareness and help young people recognize and stay away from drugs and other things that could get them into trouble.

Pamela Smart

A young man, by the name of Billy Flynn, joined "Project Self-Esteem" when he was a sophomore in high school. They got to talking about heavy metal music and realized it was something they had in common. Over time, the two of them spent more and more time together. He would go out of his way to volunteer with her and would often visit her in her office. Soon, the two of them began seeing each other in a more intimate way.

The Murder of Gregory Smart

In early May of 1990, Pamela was at work, attending a meeting. When she got home, she found her home destroyed and her husband dead. She immediately called the police. When the police arrived, they determined Greg had been shot and died instantly. As they searched the place, police assumed it was a robbery that had gone very, very wrong.

As police started talking to people, however, it became clear there was more to the story than a simple burglary. One of Billy Flynn's friends, Vance, had the gun at his house, and his father found it. His father turned it over to the police, believing it may be the murder weapon. When the police performed their investigation on it, they determined it was in fact the gun used to murder Greg Smart. Once that was determined, the investigation seemed to come together rather quickly.

They talked to Billy Flynn and he admitted Pamela Smart had put him up to it. He told the detectives all about the affair and said Pamela had threatened to stop seeing him if he didn't murder Greg. So he got several of his friends together, sneaked into the Smart house, held Greg down, and shot him. He said he was the one that did the actual shooting while the other two played lookout and drove the car.

Billy Flynn

Finally, the police had something to go on, but not quite enough to arrest Pam. They talked to another student she was close with,

Cecelia, and convinced her to wear a wire. They had hoped to catch Pamela saying something that would implicate herself in her husband's murder. After a couple of tries, Pam confessed her role to Cecelia, which was all the police needed. They came and arrested her and charged her with first degree murder.

Trial and Aftermath

During the trial, Pamela Smart maintained her innocence. She admitted to seeing and sleeping with Billy Flynn, but said the murder was all Billy's idea. She claimed Billy wanted to have her all to himself and didn't see any other way to get Gregory out of the picture. The prosecution, however, painted Pamela as the mastermind, saying her motive was to be with Billy exclusively and benefit from the $140,000 life insurance policy.

When it came time to deliberate, the jury

ultimately sided with the prosecution and found her guilty of first degree murder. She received life imprisonment for her role in the crime. Billy Flynn also received life in prison. His accomplices received thirty years, but their sentences have been reduced over the years and they have both been paroled.

While she was in jail, two of her cell mates beat her face, resulting in her having to have surgery and a metal plate to correct it. The two cell mates said she threatened to snitch on them – they have since been relocated.

Pamela is serving her sentence at the maximum-security Bedford Hills Correctional Facility for Women, Westchester County, New York. She continues to maintain her innocence. She has tried several times to appeal her case, without success.

NANCY AND RICHARD LYON

For several years, it seemed as though Nancy and Richard Lyon had a picture-perfect life. Richard was the typical all-American boy who grew up in a middle-class family in Connecticut. He got good grades, was good looking, with ginger-colored hair and olive skin. And was well-liked by his classmates and teachers. After college, he went to the Harvard School of Design for architecture. While he was there, he met Nancy Dillard , a petite woman full of cheery energy, with short dark hair and a sweet face with alabaster skin, striking jet-black eyes, and like Richard, another bright, ambitious student who wanted to study architecture.

The two soon hit it off and the relationship grew. The two felt comfortable with each other, despite the fact she was four years older than he was. They dated throughout grad school and married shortly after they graduated. Nancy had ties in Dallas, she came from an extremely wealthy Dallas family, and her father used his connections to get both of them jobs. Even though they were happy in Massachusetts, Richard and Nancy decided Dallas would be a better financial fit.

Nancy Lyon

Soon, Nancy immersed herself in her job. Even when their two children were babies,

Nancy, as a career woman, continued to work – still a somewhat controversial decision in the mid-1980s. She hired nannies and housekeepers to help take care of their growing family.

Richard, on the other hand, struggled with his career. He went through a couple of different jobs before landing one with another one of his father-in-law's associates. While working there, he became friendly with a young, blue-eyed blonde woman named Tami Ayn Gaisford.

Infidelity and Nancy's Early Life

Richard and Tami were soon in an all-out affair, and neither one bothered to hide it from Nancy. It was only a matter of time before she found out. When she did, however, she didn't place the blame on Richard or Tami. Instead, she placed the blame squarely on herself. She told herself it was because she wasn't good enough in bed or maybe Richard had an addiction to sex.

Richard Lyon

The act of blaming herself most likely comes from Nancy's childhood. While Richard had a picturesque family growing up, Nancy did not. Around the time Nancy was eleven, she had developed an incestuous relationship with her brother, Bill Jr. It is unclear if Bill forced himself onto Nancy or if it was a mutual decision, but either way, Nancy felt incredibly guilty about their relationship for many years. At some point, their parents caught them in a sexual act and sent Bill Jr. to a boarding school, increasing Nancy's guilt.

Nancy's father never acknowledged the relationship. Even years later he insisted the two of them were only playing and that nothing untoward had gone on. At one point, Nancy tried to talk about it with him and he simply shut the conversation down.

After learning of the affair, Nancy went to counseling to get over her issues with incest. As she grew stronger, she was determined to confront Richard. She canceled their joint credit cards and the business accounts he had access to. Since Richard was used to being able to spend freely, he quickly went into bankruptcy.

Nancy managed to convince her father Richard was addicted to sex and drugs, and so her father paid for Richard to attend rehab. Richard, not really caring at all, only lasted two weeks. He ended up checking himself out and going on a romantic getaway with Tami. Every time Nancy caught Richard cheating, he would beg and plead and she would end up forgiving him and taking him back.

Odd Symptoms

In 1990, Nancy had finally had enough and the pair separated. During this time, Richard and Nancy still went on regular dates, but Richard dated Tami also. Nancy started to receive anonymous gifts at her house; one of which was a bottle of wine. After Nancy drank it, she reported odd symptoms, such as nausea. A few times, when Nancy and Richard were out, Richard would bring her a drink with some white stuff floating on the top. After Nancy took a sip, she spit it out, citing a horrible taste. Richard insisted she drink it all; which Nancy refused. After the third incident, Nancy pieced it all together and became convinced Richard was trying to poison her. She expressed her concerns to her lawyer and some family members, but for some reason unknown, Nancy never went to the police.

In mid-1990, Richard asked Nancy if he could come back home. Nancy, despite her hesitations, allowed it, and the couple reconciled. During this time, however, Nancy repeatedly reported the same symptoms as before – nausea, vomiting, and diarrhea. She didn't want to place the blame on her husband, but she didn't have another explanation for her mysterious illnesses.

On January 8, 1991, Richard drove Nancy to the hospital. Nancy was in the passenger seat, doubled over and clutching her stomach. She was sick, dizzy, and in a lot of pain.

She ended up lapsing into a coma and being placed on life support. A week later, she was declared brain dead and her family made the choice to take her off the machine. She died shortly thereafter.

Her father demanded a full autopsy.

The autopsy determined Nancy had ingested over 100 times the normal level of arsenic, administered over a period of months. It caused a condition known as septic shock, which overruns the blood and shuts down the organs. The family immediately suspected Richard of poisoning his wife. The death of Nancy became a criminal investigation, and murder detectives immediately began to focus on her estranged husband: the most obvious suspect.

Investigation and Arrest

Even though suspicion on Richard was high, he was hard to track down. Just a week after Nancy's funeral, he was vacationing in Mexico with Tami. Meanwhile, the police continued their investigation. They discovered Richard had purchased arsenic and other toxic chemicals at a nearby laboratory, under the guise of needing them for work.

Richard, knowing he was under the watchful eye of the police, tried to deflect the blame. He pointed the finger at Bill Jr., because of Nancy's incestuous relationship with him. When that didn't work, he tried to blame a random coworker of Nancy's. And finally, he said it was probably Nancy herself, trying to get his attention and affection back.

Investigators, however, weren't buying it. The held a press conference where they named Richard Lyon as the number one suspect in the death of his wife. In May of 1991, Richard was finally arrested and charged with first degree murder for causing the death of Nancy.

The Trial

During the trial, the defense presented several pieces of evidence to help their case. The first was a clearly made up phone message, telling Richard that Nancy was dead and he was next. It was immediately disregarded by the prosecution as false. There were a couple of other pieces of evidence that were similarly faked and tossed out.

One piece of evidence, however, turned out to have some merit. Letters from Nancy to her father describing her relationship with her brother were brought to light and her father was finally forced to face the truth. In her letter, Nancy stated she thought Bill didn't like her because she was the reason he was made to go to boarding school and she was able to forge a somewhat happy life for herself.

The trial ended up boiling down to several key witnesses. The first was Tami, Richard's lover. She testified she knew he was married, but kept trying to convince him to leave his wife. She claimed she didn't know about the reconciliation until after Nancy had died. Richard then took the stand in his own defense.

While he was up there, he stated his same theories, and brushed off his affair with Tami as a friendship. Richard said it was Nancy's idea to buy the arsenic to help control some fire ants, a frequent problem in Texas, that had appeared on their property.

The person who sold the arsenic, however, claimed Tami was the one to pick up the chemicals, and not Nancy. The doctor at the hospital who treated Nancy testified she talked to him before she slipped into a coma. He said, she had described to him the previous poisoning incidents and said she felt her husband was trying to kill her. He said her last words were "please don't let me die".

It took the jury just over an hour to find Richard Lyon guilty of first degree murder. He was sentenced to life in prison. Richard still sits in jail, but continues to maintain his innocence. He has tried numerous times to appeal his case and even tried to file a wrongful death lawsuit against the hospital. All of which were without success.

Nancy and Richard´s daughters, Allison and Anna, were raised by the Dillard family.

O.J. SIMPSON

It's almost impossible to write about marriages ending in murder without at least bringing up the O.J. Simpson case. Even though he was acquitted of murdering Nicole Brown and Ronald Goldman, he still remains the number one suspect in their deaths. In fact, the cases have never been retried because there has been no one else even remotely suspected in the murders. For almost a year, the nation was riveted as this former football and movie star stood trial. Due to the double jeopardy law, though, since he was found not guilty of their murders, he can never be tried again.

Football and Hollywood

When O.J. was young, he developed an aptitude for sports – particularly football. He played for his junior college, where his talents were quickly noticed by a scout for the University of Southern California. The college offered him a football scholarship to come play on their team, which O.J. happily accepted. During his time there, he broke records left and right, making a name for himself in the world of sports. He won tons of awards and was recognized as one of the top college football players in the country.

After his time on the college circuit, O.J. was drafted by the Buffalo Bills. At first, the team struggled, but O.J. soon helped to turn their streak around. He single-handedly broke running records and helped the team move up in the NFL rankings. He was a true football star all the way around; in fact, he was named Player of the Year in 1973. After a few years of playing for the Bills, he was traded to the 49ers. He played two seasons with them before officially retiring from football. In 1985, due to his impressive statistics, he was inducted into the National Football Hall of Fame.

O J Simpson 1986

Using his football fame, O.J. started appearing in commercials, television shows, and movies.

An O.J Ad

It turned out he loved to act, and would do it any chance he got. He was even in line to launch his own show, Frogmen. He filmed the pilot for it and pitched it to NBC. NBC hadn't yet decided on whether or not they were going to air it when O.J. was arrested for the murders of Nicole and Ronald; this forced NBC's decision and they canceled the project.

First Marriage, Tragedy, and Infidelity

In 1967, O.J. Simpson married his first wife, Marguerite. They were together for several years and had three children together; Arnelle, Jason, and Aaren. While he was married to Marguerite, O.J. met Nicole and the two of them started a discreet affair. In 1979, however, tragedy struck the Simpson household. Aaren, just a month before her second birthday, fell into a family swimming pool and drowned. The tragedy proved to be too much for the couple and O.J. and Marguerite divorced within the year.

O.J 1990

O.J. still dated Nicole, however, except

now he was free to do so publicly. The two dated for five years before getting married. After they were married, Nicole gave birth to two children: Sydney and Justin. During this time, Nicole constantly accused O.J. of abusing her; a charge which O.J. denied emphatically. Finally, after seven years of marriage, Nicole filed for divorce.

Murder and Trial

On the night of June 12, 1994, Nicole Brown and Ronald Goldman were found stabbed to death outside of Nicole's condo. Investigators immediately suspected O.J. Simpson and urged him to come to the police station to turn himself in and confess. When that didn't happen, the police went to get him and started the now infamous low-speed pursuit of the white Ford Bronco. It was a chase that captivated the world.

If the chase and arrest of O.J. held the attention of the nation, it was nothing compared to the trial itself. Every day, people stopped what they were doing to watch Robert Kardashian, F. Lee Bailey, and Johnnie Cochran try to defend O.J. Simpson. Both sides brought countless witnesses and tried to show their side of the story. It was a trial that resulted in many outrageous moments, including O.J. "failing" to fit the glove on to his hand and several jurors being replaced due to the length of the trial. It was one of the first media circuses covering a trial and resulted in many rules and laws being placed in high profile court cases.

Despite all of the back and forth, and the seemingly overwhelming evidence, when the jury received the case, they came back and said they had unanimously found O.J. Simpson not guilty in the murders of Nicole Brown and Ronald Goldman. Over 100 million people watched the verdict, one of the largest audiences in television history.

Aftermath

After the trial, O.J. seemed to almost make a mockery of the system. He wrote a book titled "If I Did It" detailing how he would have committed the crime, if he had in fact done it. The Goldmans were outraged and sued O.J. for wrongful death on behalf of their son. The civil lawsuit, which was not televised, was successful. O.J. had to pay out damages as well as sign over any rights to the book. The Goldmans added an addendum to O.J.'s book called "He Did It".

Legal trouble was not over for O.J., however. Over the next several years, O.J. found himself in front of a judge for numerous offenses. The first was for battery and burglary; he was tried and acquitted of those charges. In 2001, O.J. was accused of drug possession and money laundering. Authorities searched his house, but were unable to come up with any evidence, so the charges were dropped.

In perhaps the most infamous incident after the murders, O.J. was arrested following a Las Vegas robbery in 2007. Officials claimed O.J., leading a group of masked men, broke into a home and stole several items at gun point. When O.J. was questioned, he admitted to breaking into the house, but stated he was only trying to take back what had been stolen from him. When asked about the gun, O.J. flat out denied having a weapon.

Most of O.J.'s accomplices agreed to testify against him in exchange for lower sentences; therefore, O.J. was officially arrested and tried for burglary, theft, coercion, and kidnapping. The jury took very little time to find O.J. guilty of these acts and sentenced him to 33 years in prison. He will not be eligible for parole until 2017, at the earliest.

KARL BLUESTONE

On Tuesday August 28, 2001, a police officer, Karl Bluestone, 36, murdered his pregnant wife, Jill Bluestone, 31, and their two young sons, Henry, 3, and Chandler, just 18-months-old, in Gravesend, Kent in the U.K before hanging himself.

At around 10:00 p.m. on the evening of August 28, 2001, Ernest Lane heard a frantic knocking on his door. Leaving his sitting room, he went to investigate. Through the glass door, he saw his next-door neighbor's little girl, Jessica Bluestone, 6, dressed in her pajamas, and looking terrified. He hurriedly opened the door to her.

She said to him,

"My daddy is hitting my mommy. Please

call the police. Daddy banged my head on the wooden floor. I cannot get mommy out of my mind. She had blood coming out of her neck. I don't want daddy to kill mommy."

Ernest hurriedly telephoned the police.

The police quickly arrived on the scene and while a policewoman went to talk to Ernest Lane and Jessica, others went next door to the Bluestone's adjoining semi-detached three-bedroom house in Marling Way, Gravesend. In the driveway, the family's Mitsubishi Shogun was parked. The first officers to arrive at the family home at about 10:30 p.m. found Jill Bluestone's body on the kitchen floor. She had 13 hammer wounds to her head and a neck injury caused by the claw end of a hammer. Lying beside her was a blood-covered hammer.

At the foot of the stairs, Henry, the couple's three-year-old son, lay dead in his pajamas in a pool of blood. He had 10 hammer wounds to his head. Injuries to his hands indicated to police that he had desperately tried to protect himself.

Upstairs, the police found 18-month-old Chandler in his crib alive but with severe head injuries. He had endured six blows to his forehead. He was rushed to the hospital but died later that night at Darent Valley hospital in Dartford. The Bluestone's eldest child, Jack, 7, was discovered on the bottom bunk in his bedroom. He was lying in the fetal position, severely injured, but alive. He survived.

In the garage at the back of the house, Karl Bluestone, 36, was found hanging from a rope. On his arms, there were several marks, which the police believed were caused by his wife putting up a desperate fight for her life.

Karl Bluestone was born in 1965 to two Labour Councillors in Gravesend Kent. He joined the Kent Police Force in 1987. To his colleagues in the force he was a "fun-loving professional," who loved his children.

Karl Bluestone

To his wife, Jill, he was a controlling abusive husband who had affairs with other women.

During the course of their stormy marriage, he had kicked Jill in the stomach whilst she was pregnant, threatened her with a meat cleaver, and on another occasion had smashed the back window of her Mercedes.

In June of 1999, Karl was arrested over a violent argument with his wife. During the row, Jessica, then five, was accidentally injured by a vase that Karl had hurled at Jill before he throttled his wife until she lost consciousness.

He was not charged after the incident as Jill refused to press charges.

During the month of August of 2001, Karl became increasingly irate and started to record Jill's telephone calls as he had become convinced that Jill, who worked for Basildon District Council as a senior manager, was having an affair with a work colleague.

Unable to take the jealousy and abuse any longer Jill told her husband on August 25th that she wanted to leave the marriage and take the children with her.

Jill told a friend that she felt increasingly fearful for her life; that Karl had said to her when she talked about ending the marriage,

"There is no divorce – the only way out is death."

On the day that Karl murdered his wife and two youngest children and the attempted murder of his eldest two children, he had joined work colleagues from the Windmill Street Police Station in Gravesend for an after-work drink before returning to the family home. Here, he settled in front of the television to watch one of his favorite programs, the police drama *The Bill*.

After the program finished, he began a blazing row with his wife, which culminated in the appalling tragedy.

Bluestone children

The Inquest

In November of 2001, an inquest was held into the murders in Gravesend County Court, in front of Coroner Roger Hatch. The coroner, after hearing all the evidence, said in his summing up that Karl Bluestone had realized his marriage was over and said,

"Whilst it cannot explain the tragedy, it perhaps gives an insight into Karl Bluestone's mind on August 28th."

He recorded verdicts of the unlawful killing for Jill Bluestone, 31, Henry, 3, and Chandler, 1, with head injuries being the cause of death. He recorded a verdict of suicide for Karl Bluestone, 36.

The two surviving children, Jessica and Jack, were taken in by relatives. How they can ever come to terms with the nightmare of that night is hard to imagine.

JESSICA McCORD AND ALAN BATES

Jessica McCord was seen as a troubled teenager; by the time she reached high school, "Goth" fashion was all the rage and she was a full-fledged member. She dressed in black clothing from head to toe and wore black make up to school. She was considered to be extremely anti-social. That's why it came as such as shock when she began to date Alan Bates. Alan was popular, well-liked, and involved in many school activities. Even though the relationship baffled those around them, they seemed to be a good fit for one another.

While she was still a teenager, Jessica became pregnant with Alan's daughter and the two were married in a hurried ceremony. They ended up graduating high school and having another daughter. Alan tried to go to college to get a better job to support his family, but it wasn't good enough for Jessica. She felt she deserved more than what Alan was able to provide and nitpicked him every chance she got.

At the time, both of them realized they were only together for their daughters, but didn't know what else to do. Alan was doing his best to keep the family together while Jessica continued to look for greener pastures. Eventually, she started dating someone outside of the marriage. When Alan discovered this infidelity, it turned out to be too much for him and he broke off the marriage.

Custody Battle

At first, Jessica fought against the divorce, but she relented and the two were at least able to be friendly enough in front of the children. They came to an agreement about custody and things seemed to settle into a routine. And then Alan met Terra.

Terra and Alan Bates

Terra and Alan were extremely happy together for a while. In fact, so much so, they decided to get married in June of 2000. Jessica was irate that Alan had found love again and began to unravel. Not to be outdone, Jessica married a man named Jeff shortly after Alan married Terra.

Jessica McCord

When that failed to get Alan's attention, Jessica went through the children to get to him. First, she tried to find excuses for the girls not to see their father. When they did see him, it was for shortened visits. Jessica absolutely did not want the girls around Terra. For a while, Alan went along with Jessica's demands so he wouldn't upset the girls, but eventually, enough was enough. He took the matters to court, who sided with Alan. The judge told Jessica to make sure Alan had his time with the girls.

Jessica ignored the judge's words. Instead, she chose not to be home when Alan was supposed to pick up the girls. Other times, she moved without giving Alan her forwarding address. Time and time again, Alan went before the court, the judge told Jessica to give Alan his time, and Jessica ignored him. Eventually, she was ordered to spend ten days in jail for violating the order. Alan, seeing the games his wife played with their children, decided to file for full custody of the girls.

The Murders

On February 15, 2002, Alan and Terra flew to Alabama from their home in Maryland to collect the girls and settle the custody matter. When they arrived at Jessica's house, however, they were greeted by a note on the door telling them to go around the back. As they reached the back door, they were greeted by Jessica, who sat them down in the living room. She then told them she was going to retrieve the girls and left.

A few seconds later, her husband, Jeff, entered the room and fired four shots into the couple, killing them both.

Jeff McCord

After the killing, Jessica and Jeff loaded the bodies into the trunk of the rental car, drove it to a field, and then set it on fire. They believed this would destroy any evidence and it wouldn't be able to be traced back to them. They then went home, cleaned the place of blood, replaced the floor tiles, and made sure there was nothing lying around that would implicate them. Once they were satisfied, they went to bed. The girls, luckily, were not at the house at this time. Jessica had arranged for them to spend the night with her mother.

The next morning, a local farmer called the authorities to report a forest fire. When police and fireman arrived, however, they discovered a burning car with the bodies of Alan and Terra inside the trunk. It took them almost no time at all to link the rental car to Alan, which therefore placed Jessica as the prime suspect in his murder. Police questioned Jeff and Jessica separately, and they both claimed Alan and Terra had never shown up to collect the girls. Though their stories were similar, there were some discrepancies that caused police to further investigate.

Police obtained a search warrant and entered into Jessica and Jeff's home. When they arrived, they saw the cover-up the two of them had tried to perform. The tiles they had replaced had been done unevenly; investigators also noticed there was new wallpaper, but it was askew. When they pulled it down, they found bullet holes behind it. It was all the evidence they needed to arrest Jeff and Jessica and charge them with first degree murder.

The Trial and Aftermath

All through the trial Jessica maintained her innocence; she took the stand in her own defense and claimed Alan tormented her throughout the years and she simply couldn't stand it anymore. When she was pressed, however, she couldn't provide the court with any specific details. As far as Jeff was concerned, the police tried to offer him a plea deal, but he refused to testify against his wife; so his case went to trial, too.

The jury didn't believe either of their defenses and on February 15, 2003, a year to the day that Terra and Alan were murdered, found them both guilty of first degree murder. Jessica was sentenced to life in prison – without parole. The jury said the only reason she didn't receive the death penalty was because of her two children. Jeff also received life imprisonment, but he will be eligible for parole in twenty-five years.

In 2003, the father's of Alan and Terra, Philip Bates and Thomas Klugh, filed a $150 million wrongful death lawsuit against Jessica and Jeff McCord.

The girls now live with Alan Bates' parents in an Atlanta suburb.

SCOTT PETERSON

Perhaps one of the most infamous cases in more recent history is the murder of Laci Peterson. Her husband, Scott Peterson, was convicted of her murder in 2004. At the time of her death, Laci was near the end of her pregnancy with their first child. The story caught the attention of the United States, and other parts of the world, as it unfolded. It has been said the Scott Peterson trial surpassed the number of viewers who watched the O.J. Simpson trial.

Early Life

Scott Peterson was the average all-American boy as he grew up. He was athletic and popular; he liked to fish, hunt, and golf. As a teenager, he tried to perfect his golf game because he wanted to try to get a scholarship. When that didn't pan out, however, he ended up at a junior college, California Polytechnic State University where he met Laci.

Laci was a, perky, attractive brunette who grew up happy and outgoing and was a popular cheerleader at her school. While at university, studying for a degree in ornamental horticulture, she met fellow student Scott, and became instantly infatuated with him. She raced home and told her parents she had met the man she planned to marry. Scott, for his part, was a little more reserved. He had recently broken up with someone and was trying to win her back when he met Laci. It took a little convincing, but Laci was able to turn his head and the two got married in August 1997. Scott was 26 years old and Laci 22 years old.

Laci aged twenty-seven

Cheating and Lies

It didn't take Scott long to become bored in his marriage to Laci. Within a year after they married, Scott began to date a young woman named Janet – only twenty years old. For Scott, Janet was a breath of fresh air because she was young, vibrant, bubbly, and she seemed to be really into Scott, a huge plus for him. In turn, Scott tried to buy Janet's affections by showering her with candy, flowers, and jewelry.

It all came to a head one night when Janet wanted to surprise Scott in the middle of the night. She went over to where he lived with Laci and a few roommates and crept into his room. When she got there, however, she was surprised to find Laci in bed with him. Scott was forced to confess his marriage, which ended the relationship with Janet. Laci, while understandably upset, chose to forgive Scott for his indiscretion.

For a while, things seemed to be on track for Scott and Laci. They worked together doing odd jobs, buying a house, and starting their life together. Laci worked with kids and wanted to have her own, but Scott was reluctant to the idea. In 2002, however, Laci became pregnant with their first child; a boy to be named Connor.

While Laci was thrilled to become a mom, Scott was extremely reserved. He told various family members he had hoped Laci would be infertile and he was not looking forward to the responsibility of a child. Many people brushed Scott off, assuming he would change his tune when he met Connor for the first time.

Scott, deciding the pressure was too much, started seeing Amber Frey behind Laci's back. Much like Janet, Scott pulled out all of the stops for Amber. He took her to fine restaurants and bought her extravagant gifts. Amber never knew Scott was married; so to her, it felt like a match made in heaven.

Amber Frey

At some point near Christmas, with Laci about seven months pregnant, friends of Amber grew suspicious of Scott. They confronted him about his marriage, which Scott denied over and over. He told them he had "lost" his wife, leaving them to assume she had died.

Suspicious Happenings

In the weeks before Laci's disappearance, Scott began to act oddly. He took out a life insurance policy in her name, convinced Laci to sell some of her jewelry, bought a boat, and bought four fake diplomas. In some ways, it would seem as though Scott was in the midst of a mid-life crisis. Investigators would later claim, however, this was Scott's way of trying to start his new life – one that would impress Amber and not include Laci.

On the morning of Christmas Eve, Scott and Laci's dog, a golden retriever, was found walking by itself down the road. The neighbor who discovered it simply returned it to the yard.

Around the same time, Scott placed a phone call to Laci asking her to pick up a last minute Christmas present – leaving the message on her voice mail. Scott then went fishing. When he returned home, he called Laci's mother and asked if she had seen Laci.

Sharon Rocha, Laci's mother, immediately called the police to report her daughter missing, and an investigation was launched. Scott, while cooperative, showed very little emotion about this whole thing – raising the cops' suspicions.

As more time went on, police put together a bit of a timeline. Although it can never be definitively proven, it is their best hypothesis as to what happened to Laci. Police believed Scott killed Laci on the evening of December 23. The next morning, he let the dog loose to make it seem like Laci had been abducted while out on a walk. He then staged the phone call and the fishing trip, and then came back home and called Laci's mother. Police theorize by the time

Scott alerted Laci's mother, Laci had been dead anywhere from 18 to 24 hours.

Over time, the police became increasingly suspicious of Scott Peterson. There were discrepancies in his statements and he couldn't provide an exact timeline of his whereabouts for those crucial 24 hours. Despite this, the police did not have enough information to arrest Scott.

Luckily, Amber Frey was willing to help the police in any way she could. She taped their phone calls and gave the investigators a lot of information. During one crucial phone conversation, Scott finally admitted that he had been married to Laci and that she was indeed missing. As they continued talking, Scott insinuated perhaps Amber had something to do with Laci's disappearance. At that point, Amber was done with Scott and she held a press conference where she stated she had never known Scott was married and she was sorry for Laci and her family. It was pretty clear even

Amber suspected Scott of murdering his wife.

In April of 2003, a hiker came across the body of a male fetus. The next day, the remains of Laci Peterson were found washed ashore just five miles from where Scott Peterson had said he went fishing. Only Laci's torso remained, her head, hands, and feet were not recovered. Police wasted no time in arresting Scott and formally charging him with murder.

The Trial

During the trial, defense attorneys for Scott Peterson tried to argue Scott was being framed by a burglar or other random abductor. They claimed there was no evidence to tie Scott to the murder and there was no motive. They also tried to state the baby had been born alive and died after he left the womb, making Scott not responsible for his death, either.

Prosecutors, however, had their secret

weapon. Amber Frey came to testify against Scott, telling all about their affair and how Scott had acted after Laci's disappearance. They claimed by putting all of the pieces of this mystery together, there was no way anyone other than Scott had killed Laci.

The jurors took seven days to come back with a guilty verdict against Scott of the second-degree murder of his unborn son Conner and the first-degree murder of his wife Laci Peterson. Scott was sentenced to death. In 2005, Laci's parents filed a wrongful death lawsuit against Scott, but ultimately dropped it in 2009.

SAN QUENTIN STATE PRISON
PETERSON, S.
V-72100
CONDEMNED   06/12/07

Ten years after his conviction, Scott Peterson, remains sitting in San Quentin prison on death row and is still appealing his conviction.

MICHAEL ROSEBERO

Michael Roseboro was great at portraying the image he wanted other people to see. To the outside world, he had a great job, a beautiful home, and a devoted, loving family with four children. His wife, Jan, seemed to be infatuated with him. His father was well-connected and got Michael work in the family business. It was a lucrative job that merited him a nice check and many friends.

Inside, however, were some well-kept family secrets. Michael had a history of lying; it started off small, but the lies eventually grew and became harder for Michael to keep straight. He developed a wandering eye and started having extra-marital affairs. There was one woman in particular, Angela Funk, who Michael developed a special interest in. In fact, he became obsessive with her, calling her and seeing her as much as he possibly could. Eventually, he wanted to be with Angela and no one else. Rather than get a divorce, he chose to murder his wife.

Jan Roseboro

On July 28, 2008, Jan Roseboro was found strangled and beaten in her swimming pool. The official cause of death was drowning. After the murder, Michael maintained his innocence, stating that he didn't do it and it must have been a burglar or someone else. When news of the affair reached investigators, however, it took them no time to arrest and charge Michael with murder.

Michael Roseboro

The trial was relatively uneventful, with most of the argument being whether the murder was premeditated or not. When the jury came back, they ended up convicting him and sentencing him to life in prison. Their reasoning was that during the strangling and the drowning, Michael Roseboro had plenty of time to think about his actions and stop at any time; he just chose not to.

CHRIS AND VICKY SORTERIOU

Chris Sorteriou had been celebrating his 44th birthday in Melbourne, Australia, when the unthinkable happened. As he and his wife were making their way back to the car after a night of fun, a man jumped out from between the cars and stabbed Chris in the neck several times. As Chris went down due to his injuries, he worried about his wife, Vicky.

Chris and Vicky Sorteriou

Chris was rushed to the hospital where a team of doctors rushed to his aid. They did all they could and they were eventually able to save his life. Although he ended up in a medically induced coma for ten days, he was able to come out of it and woke up.

As he awoke, his brother was on hand to tell him some harsh news. It wasn't a random attack in the garage; in fact, it was Chris's own wife, Vicky, who was behind it all. Chris was stunned, sad, and repeated over and over again that he wished the attack had killed him after all. He didn't want to be in a world where a woman he loved so much was capable of such a heinous crime.

He had absolutely no idea that Vicky, despite her insistence that she loved him, had been seeing another man behind his back. It was another fact in this whole twisted ordeal that stunned Chris and left him reeling. For years, he treated his wife like a queen. He showered lavish gifts on her and held her up on a pedestal. He truly believed she was the love of his life and was extremely surprised to find out she didn't feel the same way.

Vicky, not wanting to condemn herself, managed to convince the couple's daughter that Chris had organized the attack on himself in order to frame her. The investigators, however, failed to believe that story. They arrested Vicky and her lover, Ari, and charged them with attempted murder.

Throughout the trial, Vicky maintained her innocence. The jury didn't agree with her and found both her and Ari guilty of attempted murder. Vicky was sentenced to nine years in prison without the possibility of parole. Ari was sentenced to seven years, and ordered to serve five before being eligible for parole.

When asked why Vicky would want him dead, Chris speculated it was all due to the money. He said if she had divorced him, she would only get about three million dollars, but if he had died, she would have been entitled to around seven million dollars.

The trial ended in 2011, and Vicky is currently serving her sentence.

In November, 2013, Vicky lost her appeal against her conviction for attempted murder.

CONCLUSION

Divorce can be a heart wrenching and difficult thing for anyone to go through. After all, when people enter into a marriage they do so with the intention of spending the rest of their lives together. They dream of growing old and dying together. What they cannot fathom is dying before their time at the hands of the very person who promised to love them forever.

Most of the time, when people choose to get divorced, they expect to not spend any more time with their former spouses. Divorces run the gambit from the ugly and bitter, to the friendly and amicable. It all depends on the people involved, the reasons for the divorce, and the outside influences that may be involved.

People get divorced every day for all

kinds of reasons. It could be a simple set of disagreements, it could be the chemistry just flamed out, or it could be due to money or cheating spouses. People also choose to handle it in a million different ways. Some jump into a new relationship, others seek therapy or comfort, and still others hide within themselves and wallow in pity.

Some people decide to take things a step further and choose to murder their former loved one. With this, the murderer often feels like it will free them of whatever burden their spouse is forcing onto them. They feel like they can get insurance money, be free to be with whomever they want, or just get rid of a lover so they feel like they can move on. In some instances, it's because they have lost a love and they don't want anyone else to have them.

In nearly all of the cases of a deadly divorce, the signs are there well before the murder actually takes place. There are reports of stalking, threatening phone calls, or large life insurance policies being taken out. Also, in many of these cases, the murderer feels as though they cannot be caught. And sometimes, they are exactly right.

Murder cases can be difficult to prosecute, because they have to be proven beyond a reasonable doubt. That means, if even an inkling of reservation exists, the person on trial will be found not guilty. It is especially important for prosecutors to be absolutely sure they are going after the right person, because once a person is acquitted, they cannot be retried for the same crime. That's why there are several cases, even though the murder had been caught, tried, and acquitted, that remain technically unsolved.

By looking at these cases more closely, perhaps some warning signs can be seen. If a person notices a spouse acting oddly or feels someone may be in danger after a divorce, it is up to them to call the police and get the ball rolling to help prevent another senseless tragedy.

SOURCES

Marriage/Divorce Statistics:

http://www.cdc.gov/nchs/fastats/marriage-divorce.htm

http://www.foryourmarriage.org/the-truth-about-divorce-statistics/

http://www.huffingtonpost.com/tag/marriages-that-end-in-murder/

Ruth Snyder

http://en.wikipedia.org/wiki/Ruth_Snyder

http://www.prairieghosts.com/ruth_judd.html

http://murderpedia.org/female.S/s/snyder-ruth.htm

Scott Peterson

http://www.crimelibrary.com/notorious_murders/family/laci_peterson/1.html

SOURCES

http://www.dailymail.co.uk/news/article
-2202172/Pictures-details-convicted-killer-Scott-
Petersons-life-death-row--author-granted-
access-prison-time-decade.html

http://www.cnn.com/2013/10/15/us/scott-
peterson-trial-fast-facts/

Nancy and Richard Lyon

http://www.crimelibrary.com/notorious_
murders/family/richard_lyon/index.html

http://www.mirror.co.uk/tv/tv-
previews/fatal-vows-husband-who-poisoned-
1748327

http://www.texasmonthly.com/story/kill
er-next-door

http://crimeshots.com/LyonMurder.html

Michael Roseboro

http://www2.readingeagle.com/article.as
px?id=158660

http://www.thaindian.com/newsportal/e
ntertainment/michael-roseboros-girlfriend-
featured-on-television_100331213.html

Chris Sorteriou

http://www.news.com.au/entertainment/
tv/chris-soteriou-tells-sunday-night-how-his-
wife-vicky-tried-to-have-him-killed/story-
e6frfmyi-1227012425158

http://www.smh.com.au/national/chris-
soteriou-speaks-of-the-night-he-was-nearly-
murdered-by-his-wife-and-her-lover-on-
sunday-night-20140803-100214.html

ww.heraldsun.com.au/news/law-
order/kill-plot-victim-chris-soteriou-still-
struggles-with-how-to-tell-his-children-his-wife-
tried-to-kill-him/story-fni0ffnk-
1227010329270?nk=873ec529e1aa26f89ee43fb805
0bcf80

Pamela Smart

http://murderpedia.org/female.S/s/smart-
pamela.htm

http://wermenh.com/pame.html

http://www.people.com/article/billy-
flynn-pamela-smart-to-die-for-murder-case

SOURCES

Jessica McCord

http://www.murderpedia.org/female.M/
m/mccord-jessica.htm

http://truecrimezine.com/jessica-mccord/

http://mylifeofcrime.wordpress.com/2014
/06/29/deadly-duo-jeff-and-jessica-mccord-
killed-her-ex-husband-alan-bates-and-his-new-
wife-terra-bates-both-sentenced-to-life-in-
prison/

http://news.google.com/newspapers?nid
=1817&dat=20031125&id=Vj4dAAAAIBAJ&sji
d=gaYEAAAAIBAJ&pg=3159,5891603

Betty Broderick

http://www.crimelibrary.com/notorious_
murders/family/broderick/1.html

http://en.wikipedia.org/wiki/Betty_Brod
erick

http://murderpedia.org/female.B/b/brode
rick-betty.htm

Jim Sullivan

http://www.crimelibrary.com/notorious_
murders/family/dd_gone_with_the_wind/2.htm

1

http://www.mypalmbeachpost.com/news
/news/local/palm-beach-murderer-james-
sulllivan-sued-to-recove/nc5Zs/

http://en.wikipedia.org/wiki/Lita_McCli
nton

http://www.cbsnews.com/news/millionai
re-manhunt/

O.J. Simpson

http://en.wikipedia.org/wiki/O._J._Simp
son#Early_life

http://en.wikipedia.org/wiki/People_of_t
he_State_of_California_vs._Orenthal_James_Si
mpson

http://www.crimelibrary.com/notorious_
murders/famous/simpson/index_1.html

http://law2.umkc.edu/faculty/projects/ftr
ials/simpson/simpson.htm

Claus von Bülow

http://www.crimelibrary.com/notorious_
murders/family/Bülow/1.html

If you enjoyed this book, please leave a
review. Thank you in advance.

OTHER BOOKS BY SYLVIA PERRINI

FOR A FULL LIST PLEASE VISIT MS PERRINI'S AMAZON PAGE

http://www.amazon.com/s/ref=sr_pg_2
?rh=n%3A283155%2Cp_27%3ASylvia+Pe
rrini&page=2&sort=relevancerank&ie=U
TF8&qid=1411150414

STOLEN LIVES; DEADLY MOMS

ASIN:B00NQ8NYQA

ISBN-10:1502437546

ISBN-13:978-1502437549

One of the hardest things someone can
live through is the loss of a child; after all,
children are not supposed to die before their
parents do. It goes against the natural order of
things. Therefore, it is unimaginable that a

mother, who had nurtured the child inside of her for nine months, would want to take the life of their own child or children. Unfortunately, this type of heinous act is something that has occurred worldwide multiple times over in history. It has been reported that over two hundred mothers in the United States each year kill their own children

DEADLY DADS OF THE U.S

ASIN:B00N50GUOM

ISBN-10: 1494762145
ISBN-13: 978-1494762148

One of the hardest things someone can live through is the loss of a child; after all, children are not supposed to die before their parents do. It goes against the natural order of things. Therefore, it is unimaginable that someone would want to take the life of their own child or children. Unfortunately, this type of heinous act is something that has occurred multiple times over in the history of the United States.

In the profiles covered in this book, all of the dad´s had dark secrets haunting them behind closed doors. They had either lost control of their lives, or of those around them, or they were about to. These were men that craved control and they didn't know what to do without it. So they made the choice to murder.

DEADLY DADS OF THE U.K

As above but deals with father's in the U.K

ASIN:B00H14P5TY

ISBN-10:1494762145
ISBN-13:978-1494762148

WOMEN SERIAL KILLERS OF THE 17th CENTURY (WOMEN WHO KILL)

ASIN:B00BKPWKG6

This was the century when royal poison scandals sent shockwaves throughout Europe. The scandals so rocked France, that Louis XIV in

1662, passed a law stopping the sale of poisonous substances to people other than professionals, and for all purchasers to be registered.

In this short booklet of approximately 9,300 words, best selling author Sylvia Perrini takes a look at some of the most prolific women poisoners of this century, and a look at one woman, who did not use poison, just torture.

Be prepared to be shocked.

WOMEN MURDERERS OF THE 18th CENTURY (WOMEN WHO KILL)
ASIN:B007B2G0KY

Why do women kill and murder? They are supposed to be the gentler sex, the ones who nurture the babies and support families, keeping the very structure of society in place. Why do some women go wrong? Is it greed, jealousy, power or just plain wickedness?

Women Murderers have been around for

centuries. In this short book of approximately 12,500 words best selling author Sylvia Perrini looks at the profiles of eight women who operated in the 18th century.

Prepare to be shocked.

WOMEN SERIAL KILLERS OF THE 19th CENTURY: THE GOLDEN AGE OF POISONS (WOMEN WHO KILL)

ASIN:B00BK9QY2S

The 19th Century is often regarded as the heyday of poisoners. In the beginning to the middle of the nineteenth century, a poisoning panic engrossed the public imagination. In the Times newspaper in England, between 1830 and 1839, fifty-nine cases of murder by poisoning were reported. By the 1840s, the number reported had risen to hundreds. And, of these hundreds of poisonings, sixty percent involved women murderers.

In this fascinating book, best selling

author Sylvia Perrini, looks at serial women killers around the world in the 19th Century. Nearly all the cases, but not all, involve poisoning.

WOMEN SERIAL KILLERS OF THE 20th CENTURY

ASIN:B00C0JRMFA

ISBN-10: 1483953963
ISBN-13: 978-1483953960

The 20th-century, like the previous centuries, has seen no end of murders by women with poison as their choice of weapon. Furthermore, just like in the previous centuries, the murders have been just as cold and calculating.

Those lucky few who have managed to survive an attempted murder by these women have described being poisoned as being equal to being devoured alive.

However, the 20th century has also seen

murders committed by women with guns and, in the case of Dana Gray, with physical violence. Dana is a rarity among women serial killers, in both her choice of victim and her hands-on method of using her hands, a cord or rope, and an object with which to batter her victim.

Yet, even after all this time, we are left with the same question: what leads a woman to commit serial murder?

In this book, the author examines the profiles of twenty-five women serial killers, all of whom acted alone.

Ms. Perrini has not included mothers who solely kill their own children, as she believes that is a subject that deserves to be written about entirely separately.

Even leaving those specific types of Women Serial Killers aside, there are still many women who choose to commit murder again, and again, and again...

Welcome to the world of 20th century

women serial killers.

OR BUY THE ABOVE FOUR BOOKS IN ONE

WOMEN SERIAL KILLERS THROUGH TIME Boxed Set (4 in 1)

ASIN: B00C3N7BFY

ISBN-10: 1484044266
ISBN-13: 978-1484044261

ANGELS OF DEATH; NURSES WHO KILL (WOMEN SERIAL KILLERS)

ASIN:B00946F178

ISBN-10: 1501093096
ISBN-13: 978-1501093098

In this book, historian and best selling author Sylvia Perrini looks at some cases of serial killers, all of whom were female nurses. The crimes of these nurses are heinous and shocking.

Luckily, nurses, who murder their

patients, are the exception. They are not the rule. However, the number of cases of nurses accused and convicted of murdering patients is rising. It's almost enough to give you a phobia about going into hospital!!

I DON'T LIKE MONDAYS: FEMALE RAMPAGE KILLERS (WOMEN WHO KILL)

ASIN:B00CW16O28

The Famous hit song "I don't like Mondays" penned by Bob Geldof, was written after the school shootings in San Diego, California, committed by Brenda Spencer. Once she was apprehended and asked why she had done it. Her reply was:

"I don't like Mondays, do you?"

When one thinks of spree killers or rampage killers, normally one thinks of a male. Men such as the Aurora Colorado Movie Theater James Eagan Holmes, Seung-Hui Cho Virginia Tech Massacre, Columbine school killers Eric

David Harris and Dylan Bennet Klebold, Adam Lanza at Sandy Hook Elementary School, and the 2011 massacre at a summer camp in Norway, by Anders Behring Breivik to name just a few.Yet, women have also committed these crimes just not in such large numbers as men

SUGAR N`SPICE: TEEN GIRLS WHO KILL (FEMALE KILLERS)

ASIN:B00DESV62Q

ISBN-10: 149045845X
ISBN-13: 978-1490458458

Murder is horrific whenever it happens and in what ever circumstances. But when a murder is carried out by a young girl, not much more than a child, it is doubly horrific.

What is it that goes wrong in the lives and minds of these girls that grow up to be teenage killers? Girls who ruthlessly murder strangers, young children, parents, and others?"

In this short book of approximately 25,000

words Sylvia Perrini has selected seven murder cases committed by teenage girls. The profiles of the girls covered are;

PAULINE PARKER AND JULIET HULME aka Anne Perry, the well-known author of murder fiction.

BRENDA ANN SPENCER

CHERYL PIERSON

HOLLY HARVEY AND SANDRA KETCHUM

CHELSEA O'MAHONEY

CINDY COLLIER AND SHIRLEY WOLF

ALYSSA BUSTAMANTE

OR BUY THE ABOVE THREE BOOKS IN ONE

WOMEN WHO KILL (3 books in 1) Rampage Killers, Teens Who Kill & Nurses Who Kill)

ASIN: B00DHT1C1W

NO, DAD! PLEASE, DON'T! (THE

ASIN: B00EI2BA28

ISBN-10: 149482728X
ISBN-13: 978-1494827281

On the morning of December the 8th, 1971, New Jersey, and indeed the entire metropolitan New York City area, awoke to lurid newspaper headlines of the horrific massacre of almost an entire family in the affluent community of Westfield, N.J.; a story that both captivated and horrified a nation. The story was quickly picked up around the world.

The face of John List, who had left letters confessing to the crime, stared out at the readers. He was an ordinary, fairly non-descript looking man. The question on everyone's lips as news broke of the horrific slaughter by a college-educated, seemingly successful accountant, and Sunday school teacher was why? He had murdered his mother, wife and three teenage children.

In this short booklet, of approximately 11,000 words, best selling author, Sylvia Perrini, delves into the events that led to the horrific slaughter of John Lists, mother, wife and three teenage children.

John List managed to evade capture for over 18 years and never expressed remorse for his crimes.

BABY FARMERS OF THE 19th CENTURY (WOMEN WHO KILL)

ASIN:B00ACPGTFI

BABY FARMERS OF THE 19th CENTURY

The practice of baby farming came about in late Victorian times. In this era, there was a great social stigma attached to having a child out of marriage and no adequate contraception existed. In this period of time, no child protection services or regulated adoption agencies were in existence.

A number of untrained women offered adoption and fostering services to unmarried mothers who would hand over their baby and a cash payment. The mothers hoped that this payment would find stable, happy homes for their babies. And in the case of weekly payments that they would at some time in the future be able to re-claim their child.

It was, without doubt, one of the most sickening aspects of Victorian times, not only in Britain but also in its colonies as well.

Many of these fostering and adoption agencies were bona fide, but a frightening number were not. They became known as baby farms.

In this short book, best selling author, Sylvia Perrini, introduces us to some of these baby farmers.

FIVE WOMEN SERIAL KILLER PROFILES; Boxed Set

ASIN:B00A9HW3KO

This is a compilation of best-selling author, Sylvia Perrini's, five short books of Women Serial Killers.

The profiles contained in this volume are:

DOROTHEA HELEN PUENTE-SOCIAL WORKER'S SAVIOR!!

VELMA BARFIELD- GATEWAY TO HEAVEN

GENENE JONES-CODE BLUE

AILEEN WUORNUS-DAMSEL FOR SALE

KATHLEEN FOLBIGG--UNJUST JUSTICE?

Some of these stories will shock you to the core, and some may make you weep. They may also be bought separately.

SERIAL KILLERS TRUE CRIME ANTHOLOGY 2014 (Annual Anthology)[Kindle Edition]

Sylvia Perrini (Author),Peter

Vronsky(Author),Michael
Newton(Author), RJ Parker
(Author),Dane Ladwig(Author)

Publication Date:December 15, 2013

ASIN:B00H7LQU40

ISBN-10:1494325896
ISBN-13:978-1494325893

WARNING: This book contains forensic crime scene evidence photographs and statements that some may find disturbing.

Serial killers; they cross the bounds of evil. They murder at random without logic or reason other than the one twisting in their sick and evil minds. They are diabolical vile creatures devoid of morality or pity. You will meet a chosen few of them in these pages. We will see that serial killers are roaming among us all, from small towns to big cities. They are not limited to a particular place, gene pool, culture, social class or religion. They are not restricted to any particular demographic, political propensity and they can be of any gender.

Some of the serial killers chosen for this first annual Serial Killers True Crime Anthology you might have heard of and we present their tales in new ways. Others have not graced every newspaper, tabloid or television screen and represent tales of true crime horror told in detail for the first time in these pages. Five of true crime's most prolific authors have come together in these pages to present their most compelling cases of serial homicide, famous and not so famous.

OTHER GOLDMINE GUIDE PUBLICATIONS

SAILING INTO THE ABYSS (TRUE SMUGGLING ADVENTURE) (MARIJUANA SMUGGLING)

BRIDGET LANE

ASIN:B009N1IRSE

ISBN-10: 1480257001

ISBN-13: 978-1480257009

This is a life-changing true story of drug-running across the Pacific. A young girl, with a passion for sailing and adventure, gets approached to transport an illegal cargo from Colombia to the US, a journey that plunges her into an adventure that will test her courage like no other. She battles with storms, snakes, and interminable days at sea, whilst facing deprivations barely imaginable, before finally being intercepted by a Mexican gunboat in waters infested with Great White Sharks.

Her subsequent incarceration in Mexico's most infamous prison, La Mesa, is almost more surprising: the treatment she receives and the people she meets become a transformative experience, as she recounts in this totally compelling personal journey.

This is truly an extraordinary adventure story of a remarkable young woman operating in a man's world.

WOMEN PIRATES (SCANDALOUS WOMEN)
ANNA MYERS
ASIN:B007KQCBF4

There is an old superstition among sailors that women at sea bring bad luck. Despite this, many women have proved their seafaring skills. When we think of Pirates we have a tendency to think of masculine men. But did you know that the most successful pirate of all time was a woman? Neither the Chinese, British or Portuguese navies could stop her. In this delightful short book author Anna Myers takes a look at the lives of eight wicked women pirates.

DESERT QUEEN; LADY HESTER STANHOPE (SCANDALOUS WOMEN)
ANNA MYERS
ASIN:B00BAKB4XQ

In this wonderful short book, author Anna Myers looks at the colorful life of the extraordinary bohemian adventuress Lady Hester Stanhope.

Lady Hester lived in England until the age of about 34 when she set off traveling and fell in love with the Middle East. While en route to Egypt she was shipwrecked, and lost all her clothes. Unable to purchase European clothes she adopted a male version of Turkish dress. This, made her a bit of a 'cause celeb' in the

Middle East, and also that she rode horseback into Damascus without a veil, an unthinkable thing to do at the time. In fact, many of the things Lady Hester did were unthinkable at the time, which is what made her such a colorful character.

Many of the travels she undertook were exceedingly dangerous, but she appeared fearless. She was the first European woman - and one of the few Europeans to survive the dangerous journey - to enter Palmyra, in the middle of the Syrian desert. The native Bedouins crowned her as "Queen of the Desert". Hester chose to settle down in Lebanon, where she became a local folk hero, offering shelter to those affected by wars and the battles for supremacy in the region.

When the British Government, under Lord Palmerston, stopped her pension, she died in her home in Djoun, destitute, friendless and alone.

SCANDALOUS LADIES (WICKED WOMEN)

ANNA MYERS

ASIN:B007S9YCIM

Author Anna Myers in this delightful short book, provides a gallery of extraordinary women swindlers, con artists and imposters. Some of the women you may even like and some you will despise.

MARTHE HANAU

'La Banquière'

POILLON SISTERS

Sisters you wouldn't want to meet on a dark night.

ELIZABETH BIGLEY

The Enterprising Mrs. Chadwick

THÉRÈSE HUMBERT

ANN O'DELIA DISS DEBAR

"One of the most extraordinary fake mediums and mystery swindlers the world has ever known".

ANNA SCHNEIDER

Too Many Husbands Spoil The Broth

ELLEN PECK

Just never wanted to retire!

BERTHA HEYMAN

"One of the smartest confidence women
in America"

SARAH RACHEL RUSSELL

'The Beautician from Hell'

SARAH WILSON

Princess of Mecklenburg-Strelitz sister?

ANNA ANDERSON

Was she Czar Nicolas's II daughter ?

PRINCESS CARABOO

The greatest actress of all time!

LOVE YOUR LIVER:How to keep your
liver healthy (HEALTHY LIVING)

PENNY LANE

ASIN:B0077SP1SO

This book has some great tips for good liver health, delicious liver-friendly recipes and information that will help you get to know one of your most hardworking and vital organs. The liver performs an amazing 500 different functions. It produces bile, essential for breaking down fat for absorption and extracting vitamins A, D, E and K, stores energy from food until it is needed, and aids our natural immunity by releasing chemicals to fight infection.With so many important jobs to do, your liver is robust enough to carry on even when it is damaged - it can even repair itself. But every organ has its limits and the liver is no exception. We must learn to love our liver. Our liver helps us to recover from all our over indulgence's. So learn to give your liver the love it deserves, and this book will help you do so.

FISH AND SEAFOOD FOR LOVE (NATURE'S NATURAL

ASIN:B00DKE6TLM

The ancient world believed seafood had aphrodisiac characteristics because, the Greek goddess of love, Aphrodite, sprang from the foam of the sea on an oyster shell (hence Botticelli's much reproduced painting of the goddess floating on a seashell). The Romans named her Venus.

The sea is one of the major sources of life and Seafood has been seen as the food of love for many centuries. A claim that is not surprising considering it is brimming with minerals such as calcium, zinc, iodine and iron.

In this delightful book of aphrodisiac foods, the author looks at the most popular fishy aphrodisiacs as well as providing some excellent recipes to enjoy them.

16450696R00097

Printed in Great Britain
by Amazon